meet the family

my Brother

by Mary Auld

W

FRANKLIN WATTS

LONDON•SYDNEY

This is Emma and her brother James with their mum and dad. James is five years younger than his sister Emma.

Nasser's brother is just
a baby. Nasser sometimes
holds him – very carefully.

Heather's brother is her twin. They were born 15 minutes apart.

Claire's older brother David has a different dad.
He is her half-brother.

Steve and Michael are step-brothers. Steve's mum is married to Michael's dad now – but they had Steve and Michael with other people before they met.

Zoe's brother goes
to nursery school.

Andy's brother
has a Saturday job.

Li's brother has
a computer.
He lets Li use it.

Ed likes to do acrobatics
with his brother.

Sometimes Rachel and her brother fight.

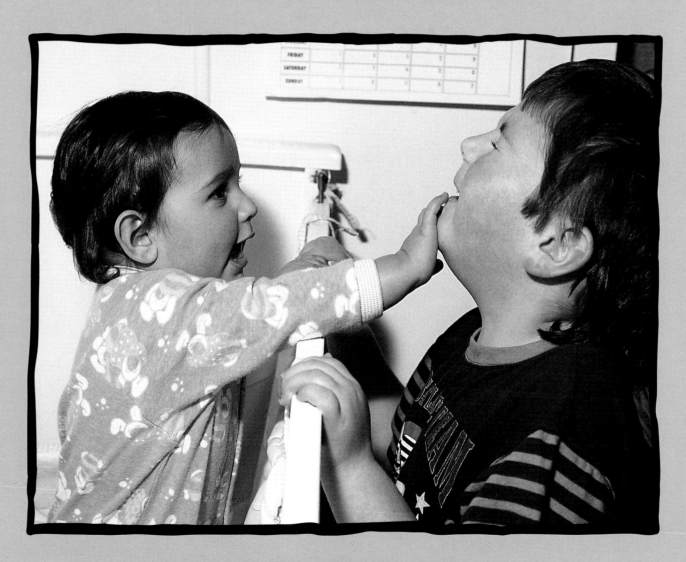

Louise has bike races
with her two brothers.

Molly and her brothers make camps in their back garden.

This is Scot with his mum
and his mum's brother —
Scot's Uncle Carl.

Do you have a brother?
What's he like?

Family words

Here are some words people use when talking about their brother or family.

Names for children:
Brother, Sister; Son, Daughter.

Names for parents:
Father, Daddy, Dad, Pa;
Mother, Mummy, Mum, Ma.

Names of other relatives:
Grandchildren; Grandparents;
Grandmother, Granny, Grandma;
Grandfather, Grandad, Grandpa;
Uncle; Aunt, Auntie; Nephew, Niece.

If we put the word 'Step' in front of a relative's name, it means that we are related to them by marriage but not by birth.

If we put the word 'Half' in front of our brother or sister, it means that one of our parents is the same and the other is different.

A family tree

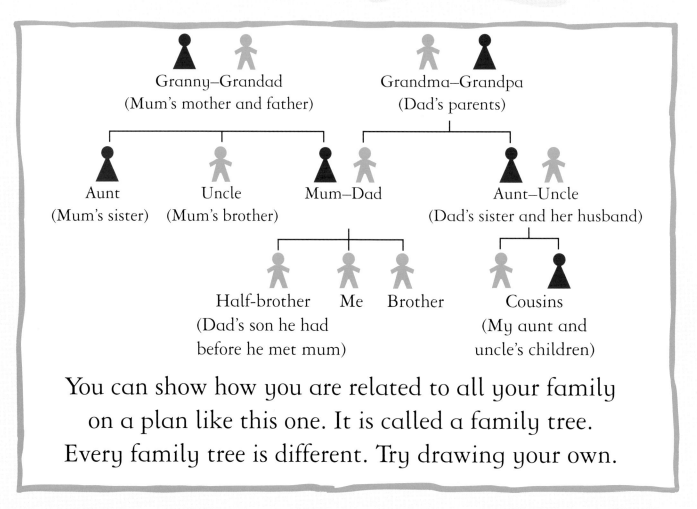

Granny–Grandad
(Mum's mother and father)

Grandma–Grandpa
(Dad's parents)

Aunt
(Mum's sister)

Uncle
(Mum's brother)

Mum–Dad

Aunt–Uncle
(Dad's sister and her husband)

Half-brother
(Dad's son he had
before he met mum)

Me

Brother

Cousins
(My aunt and
uncle's children)

You can show how you are related to all your family
on a plan like this one. It is called a family tree.
Every family tree is different. Try drawing your own.

First published in 2003 by Franklin Watts,
96 Leonard Street, London EC2A 4XD

Franklin Watts Australia
45-51 Huntley Street, Alexandria, NSW 2015

Copyright © Franklin Watts 2003

Series editor: Rachel Cooke
Art director: Jonathan Hair
Design: Andrew Crowson

A CIP catalogue record for this book
is available from the British Library.

ISBN 0 7496 4886 4

Printed in Hong Kong/China

Acknowledgements:
Bruce Berman/Corbis: front cover centre
below. www.johnbirdsall.co.uk: front cover
main, 1, 5, 12, 18, 22. Craig Hammell/
Corbis: 9. Judy Harrison/Format: 17. Carlos
Goldin/Corbis: front cover centre above. Sally
Greenhill, Sally & Richard Greenhill: 16, 19.
Ronnie Kauffman/Corbis: 20. Peter Olive/
Photofusion: 13. Gary Parker/Photofusion: 6.

Jose Luis Pelaez/Corbis: front cover centre top,
14. George Shelley/Corbis: front cover bottom.
Ariel Skelley/Corbis: front cover centre. Bob
Watkins/Photofusion: 11. Lisa Woollett/
Format: 2.